English Foundation Plus

Activity Book A

Published by Collins
An imprint of HarperCollins*Publishers*
The News Building, 1 London Bridge Street,
London, SE1 9GF, UK

HarperCollins Publishers
Macken House, 39/40 Mayor Street Upper,
Dublin 1, D01 C9W8, Ireland

Browse the complete Collins catalogue at
www.collins.co.uk

ISBN 978-0-00-846860-6

British Library Cataloguing-in-Publication Data
A catalogue record for this publication is available from the British Library.

Author: Fiona Macgregor
Publisher: Elaine Higgleton
Product manager: Letitia Luff
Commissioning editor: Rachel Houghton
Edited by: Hannah Hirst-Dunton
Editorial management: Oriel Square
Cover designer: Kevin Robbins
Cover illustrations: Jouve India Pvt. Ltd.
Internal illustrations: Jouve India Pvt. Ltd.,
p 2–5, 15–16 Priya Kuriyan
Typesetter: Jouve India Pvt. Ltd.
Production controller: Lyndsey Rogers

Printed in India by Multivista Global Pvt. Ltd.

Acknowledgements

With thanks to all the kindergarten staff and their schools around the world who have helped with the development of this course, by sharing insights and commenting on and testing sample materials·

Calcutta International School: Sharmila Majumdar, Mrs Pratima Nayar, Preeti Roychoudhury, Tinku Yadav, Lakshmi Khanna, Mousumi Guha, Radhika Dhanuka, Archana Tiwari, Urmita Das; Gateway College (Sri Lanka): Kousala Benedict; Hawar International School: Kareen Barakat, Shahla Mohammed, Jennah Hussain; Manthan International School: Shalini Reddy; Monterey Pre-Primary: Adina Oram; Prometheus School: Aneesha Sahni, Deepa Nanda; Pragyanam School: Monika Sachdev; Rosary Sisters High School: Samar Sabat, Sireen Freij, Hiba Mousa; Solitaire Global School: Devi Nimmagadda; United Charter Schools (UCS): Tabassum Murtaza and staff; Vietnam Australia International School: Holly Simpson

The publishers wish to thank the following for permission to reproduce photographs.

(t = top, c = centre, b = bottom, r = right, l = left)

p 18 Will Amlot

The publishers gratefully acknowledge the permission granted to reproduce the copyright material in this book. Every effort has been made to trace copyright holders and to obtain their permission for the use of copyright material. The publishers will gladly receive any information enabling them to rectify any error or omission at the first opportunity.

Extracts from Collins Big Cat readers reprinted by permission of HarperCollins*Publishers* Ltd

All © HarperCollins*Publishers*

MIX
Paper | Supporting responsible forestry
FSC™ C007454

This book contains FSC™ certified paper and other controlled sources to ensure responsible forest management.

For more information visit: www.harpercollins.co.uk/green

T0321878

Trace

I am me!

Trace over the dotted lines.

Date:

Match

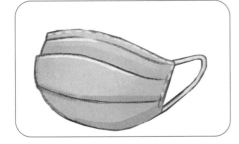

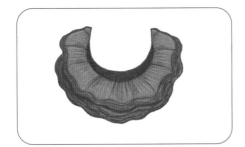

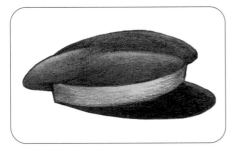

Match the thing to the person.
Draw a line to join them.

Date:

Trace

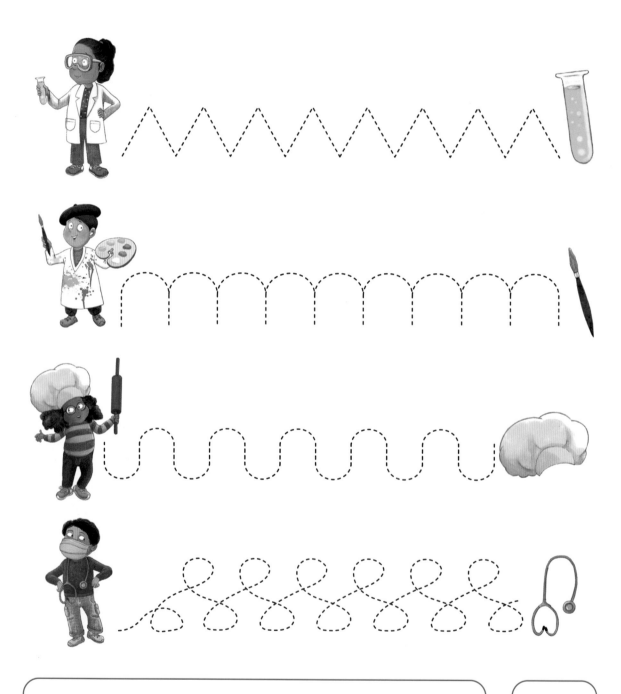

Trace over the dotted lines to help the people
find their things.

Date:

Trace and say

ink

Trace the letter. Say the sound. Say the word.

Date:

Count

2

3

4

5

6

Trace the numbers. Draw a line to match each
number to the correct family.

Date:

Trace and say

mum

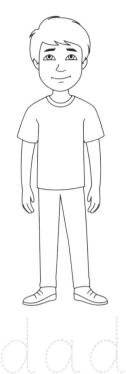

dad

baby

me

Trace the letters. Say the sounds.
Say the words.

Date:

Draw

Draw a picture of some people in your family.
Write their names if you can.

Date:

Colour

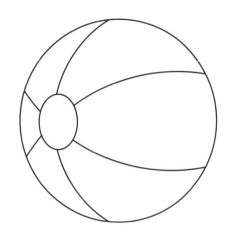

Colour all the things that start with the 'a' sound.

Date:

Trace and say

apple

a a a a

a a a a

a

A A A A

A A A A

A

Trace the letter. Say the sound. Say the word.

Date:

Circle

I taste

Circle the foods you like to taste. Trace the letters.

Date:

Colour

Colour the things you like to smell.

Date:

Draw

What can you hear in the classroom and outside?
Draw what is making the noises you can hear.   Date:

Trace and say

sun

Trace the letter. Say the sound. Say the word.

Date:

Put in order

1 2 3 4

Number the pictures to match
the order of the story.

Date:

Find

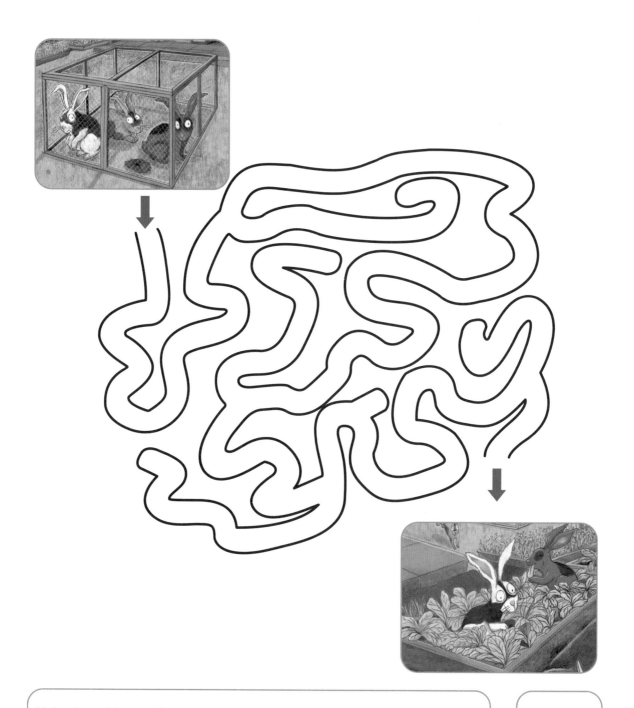

Help the rabbits to find their way to the vegetables.

Date:

Trace and say

nest

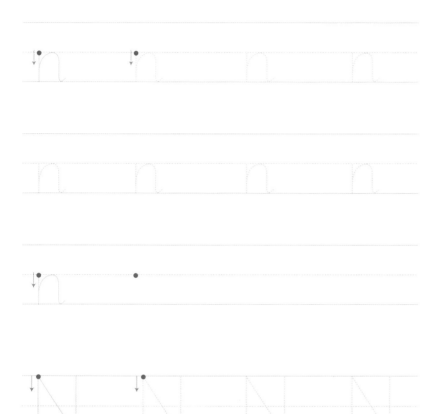

Trace the letter. Say the sound. Say the word.

Date:

Put in order

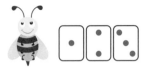

1 2 3 4

plant

pat

pot

pit

Number the pictures to match the order of the story.
Use the numbers 1 to 4. Say the words.   Date:

Trace and say

pot

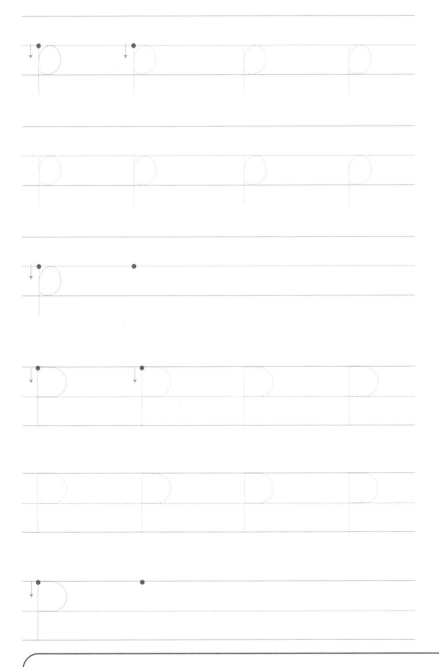

Trace the letter. Say the sound. Say the word.

Date:

Match

Match the parts to the plant.

Date:

Trace and say

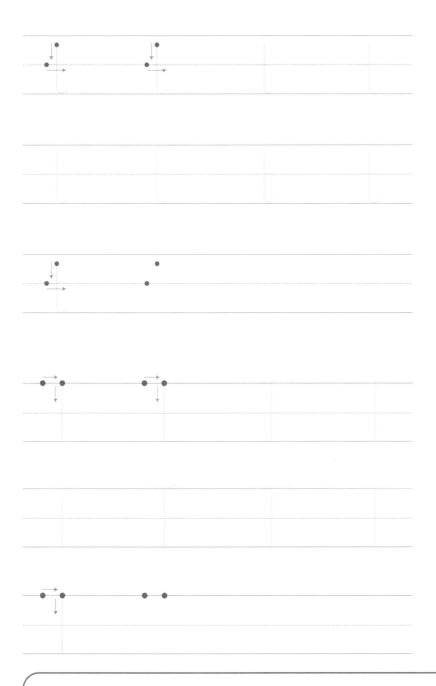

tap

Trace the letter. Say the sound. Say the word.

Date:

Alphabet time

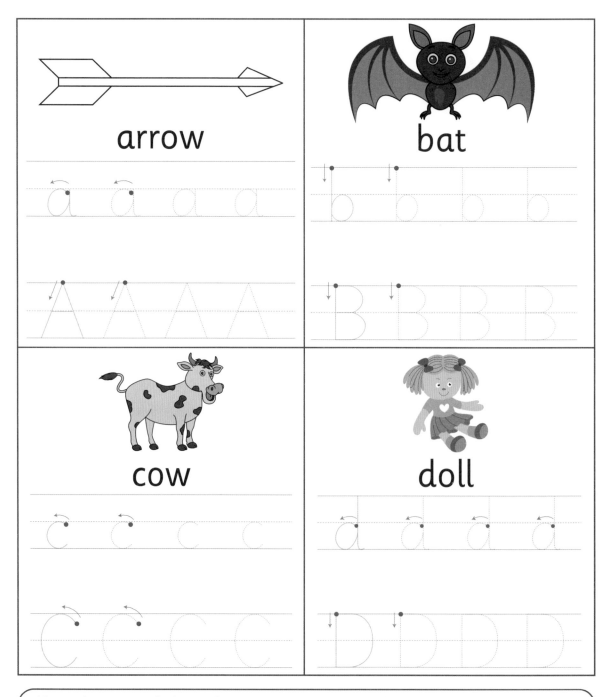

arrow

bat

cow

doll

Alongside structured phonics lessons, you may want to display and talk about one letter of the alphabet in an 'alphabet time' session each week.

Alphabet time

elephant

fork

gift

horse

Alongside structured phonics lessons, you may want to display and talk about one letter of the alphabet in an 'alphabet time' session each week.

Assessment record

_____ has achieved these English Foundation Plus Objectives:

Reading

R1 Develop an increasing awareness of sound structures in language	1	2	3
R2 Consolidate and develop early reading skills	1	2	3
R3 Recognise more letters of the English alphabet, and their corresponding sounds	1	2	3
R4 Begin to use phonemes to read single-syllable words with short vowels	1	2	3
Reading motor skills	1	2	3

Writing

W1 Consolidate and develop early writing skills	1	2	3
Writing motor skills	1	2	3

Speaking

S1 Be able to express oneself in a range of everyday situations	1	2	3
S2 Sentences and words: begin to segment and blend	1	2	3
Speaking developmental skills	1	2	3

Listening

L1 Know how to listen and respond appropriately in a range of everyday contexts	1	2	3
Listening developmental skills	1	2	3

1: Partially achieved
2: Achieved
3: Exceeded

Signed by teacher:
Signed by parent: Date: